The Lace Dealer's Pattern Book

Compiled by Veronica Main

Curator
Luton Culture

A **Luton Culture** Publication

Acknowledgements

The Friends of Luton Museums have generously supported re-publication of the Lace Dealer's Pattern Book by funding new high resolution scans of the conserved sheets. We offer them grateful thanks for their continuing support.

Luton Culture would like to thank Glenys French, Enid Orchard, Janet Tarbox, founder members of Friends of Luton Lace, Barbara Brooks and Pat Hoath of Mainly Lace for sharing their knowledge to provide information about the samples contained within the Lace Dealer's Pattern Book.

This publication has been financed by the profits from the sale of the Lace Dealer's Pattern Book published in 1998. In honour of those who originally contributed to both the conservation work of the Pattern Book and its subsequent publication, we have included a list of donors on pages 94 and 95.

The 1998 version of the Lace Dealer's Pattern Book was compiled by Alison Taylor who was at that time Curator of Costume for Luton Museum Services. We would like to acknowledge her research and dedication to the project. Some text produced by Alison and published in the 1998 book has been reproduced herein.

Designed by Luton Culture

Published by Luton Cultural Services Trust,
Luton Central Library,
St. George's Square,
Luton,
LU1 2NG

Printed by M-Press UK Limited,
103 Station Road,
Ampthill,
MK45 2RE

DVD reproduced by DVD Plus Limited,
18-26 Latimer Road,
Luton,
LU1 3UZ

ISBN: 978-0-9573686-0-6

An East Midlands pillow-lace maker from a watercolour in the museum collection. Artist unknown.

The Lace Dealer's Pattern Book

As a result of fundraising efforts by the Lacemakers' Circle, Arachne and many lacemakers, the Lace Dealer's Pattern Book containing images of forty newly conserved sheets, was published in 1998.

The book proved very popular with lacemakers and two print runs were produced. In 2008 the last copy was sold. Since then lacemakers from around the world have continued to enquire about its availability indicating that we should republish the book.

Lacemakers enjoyed and appreciated the 1998 version but told us that its size made it too large to place on a book shelf and cumbersome to use. Respecting these comments we made the decision to commission new high quality scans of the conserved sheets and reprint the book in a smaller format with an accompanying DVD. Now larger images of the lace can be enjoyed at leisure.

This new book includes images of all forty-two sheets of lace samples from the original book which were conserved by the Textile Conservation Centre. Also included for the first time is some information about the samples shown on each sheet, and a simple challenge which invites the reader to find detail within the samples. If you look carefully you will find fine points that we have not mentioned. We hope you will enjoy this element of the new book.

The original Pattern Book had deteriorated to the point where it could not be used for research.
© Textile Conservation Centre Foundation

The Pattern Book's History

In 1955 Thomas Wyatt Bagshawe, a businessman in Dunstable, Bedfordshire gave Wardown Park Museum a collection of lace samples in a binder. Thomas Bagshawe was a knowledgeable and enthusiastic collector of both the tools and products of local traditional industries. When Luton Museum and Art Gallery opened in 1927 he loaned his large personal collection and later presented it as a donation.

In 1952 he bought the Lace Dealer's Pattern Book from Miss F E Haines, who was about to retire from her needlework supplies business in The Arcade, Bedford. Miss Haines was the last proprietor of the firm which had been built up by the lace dealer Thomazin (Thomas) Lester and later run by his sons, Thomas and Charles.

The Pattern Book contained many small samples of East Midlands, Buckinghamshire, Bedfordshire and Northamptonshire lace. The samples varied in size, design and date, but were broadly grouped by type within the book. Straight-edged insertions occupied two pages and designs with wire ground another two. The complex floral patterns of the 1840s and 1850s were mounted separately from the simpler patterns of the early 1800s. These often consisted of little more than a gimp thread running through the ground or net.

There were also piece goods, probably the ends of collars, cuffs and caps, but the majority of designs were edgings and insertions to be sold by the yard. Although Bagshawe originally believed the patterns ranged between 1854 and 1893, further research later suggested they were made between 1820 and the end of the 1890s. Eight pages contain a type of Bedfordshire lace, without a ground which was made from the 1850s onwards.

Books like this were probably intended to show the lace dealer's customers the range of designs available. They may have also provided a reference source to inspire pattern development. The Lester business may have acquired and included some patterns from other dealers who were no longer working. The Cecil Higgins Art Gallery in Bedford has an album of lace samples which seems to have originated from a dealer in Olney, Buckinghamshire, but which subsequently belonged to Thomas Lester.

Thomas Bagshawe bought the Luton Pattern Book for ten pounds. The sheets were in a leather binder along with a smaller sample book of silk blonde lace and a number of papers and patterns. Most of the papers were associated with the Wellingborough area of Northamptonshire and included blank bill heads and personal documents relating to John Spencer (1830-1895), who was a lace dealer in the town from about 1850 until about 1880. Perhaps the book had belonged to Spencer before being acquired by the Lesters who in turn passed it to Miss Haines.

After the Pattern Book entered the Luton lace collection it became an important source of design and technical information for hobby lacemakers. In the 1980s thirty-three full-size copies of the original sheets were produced and sold by the museum. They were bought by enthusiasts around the world and used by leading lacemakers to draft prickings and include them in their publications. Their work enabled others to make copies of the original pieces.

When the original book was eventually examined by conservators they found fibres from different coloured threads attached to some samples suggesting they had been remounted from an earlier book or books and probably had not come from the same source.

Some lace samples had become discoloured by the glues used during the book's life.
© Textile Conservation Centre Foundation

The Pattern Book Appeal

In 1994 conservators at the Textile Conservation Centre, then based at Hampton Court, were commissioned to carry out a survey of the costume and textile collection held at Wardown Park Museum. They found the Pattern Book was in a fragile state with many samples detached from the pages. They recommended that it should not be handled by researchers until remedial conservation had been carried out. The cost of this work was estimated at £8,000, a sum which the museum had little hope of finding from its own budgets. It seemed that the book would become a lost resource.

Shortly afterwards the Lacemakers' Circle Committee were told of the problem. They decided that, subject to the agreement of their membership, the Circle would make every effort to raise the necessary finance to conserve the Pattern Book. At the Annual General Meeting the members launched a major fund raising campaign through local groups and individual members. The first contribution was a generous donation from the Circle's own funds.

The campaign also came to the attention of a group of lacemakers organised on the Internet in 1995 under the name of Arachne. Their publicity reached lacemakers worldwide and the substantial funds raised were used for the 1998 publication.

In the remarkably short time of just eighteen months donations to the appeal had reached, and even surpassed the target. The Pattern Book was taken to the Textile Conservation Centre in the summer of 1996 and the work was completed by Christmas of the same year.

The 1998 edition of the Pattern Book included a list of the donors and we have decided it is appropriate to include that list in this publication as a continuing tribute to their efforts.

Working slowly and with great care a conservator gently eases a lace sample from the original sheet.
© Textile Conservation Centre Foundation

The Conservation Work

When the Pattern Book was given to the museum it consisted of small samples of lace glued to sheets of coarse dark paper, contained within a loose binder. Some sheets had the lace samples mounted onto both sides. Samples had come loose and their original placement was not always obvious. The sheets were larger than the leather binder and it appeared the two had not originally belonged together. Over the years the papers had become increasingly discoloured and brittle and the lace samples were stained by the chemicals leaking from the paper and glue. It was necessary to transfer them to a new and more robust backing which would cause no further damage.

Before doing anything else the conservation team made a photographic record of the book. With so many small samples, some of them being very similar, it was important to ensure that where possible the samples went back into the same place, however, that was not always possible. The pages were soaked in warm water and the lace carefully detached. Each sample was rinsed several times to remove old glue; the more stubborn adhesives were treated with acetone.

When the lace samples were clean they were remounted onto sheets of blue archival board. Each sheet was pasted with an archival quality adhesive that would not harm the lace, and the dampened lace was laid onto it. After drying out under weights, the pages were framed with a border of the same card to make the sheets more rigid and to protect the surface of the lace. The sheets were then placed in specially made polyester sleeves for protection.

The conservation work has provided researchers with visibly cleaner samples, although some are still discoloured as a result of their earlier mounting. The samples are firmly attached to the boards, properly stretched and no longer distorted by fraying and curling edges. The number of sheets has increased to forty-two due to the reattachment of the loose samples, repositioning of samples and the addition of two sheets of black lace samples.

This lappet is on sheet 14 at position 3.a.

Sheet reference numbers

To accompany the image on each sheet we have referred to details of specific samples. To locate the sample use the following system.

The vertical line number is counted from the left hand side of the sheet.

The position letter for each line is counted from the top edge towards the bottom edge of the sheet.

Sheet 1

The samples on this page are well made examples of Buckinghamshire point, also known as Bucks point. There are some very fine examples of cloth work. These laces were expensive products to buy and timely to make.

Points of interest

Line 1
1.b incorporates an unusually large area of whole stitch.

Line 2
2.c the gimp thread dissects each honeycomb filling within the leaf.

Line 3
3.b the spider inside the flower centres is Torchon style.

Your challenge

Can you find the gimped tallies?

Sheet 2

All the samples on this page are examples of Buckinghamshire, or Bucks point, ground with gimp threads forming the flowers and leaves. Two samples do not have a footside and may have been designed to attach to machine net.

Points of interest

Lines 1 and 2
1.d and 2.b incorporate an unusually random gimp line which may indicate they were designed by the same person.

Line 5
5.c two samples. These lack the expertise of the other samples on the page and may have been made by less experienced workers.

Your challenge

Can you find a Mayflower filling?

Sheet 3

The sheet contains a mixture of Bucks point and Bedfordshire samples. There are a range of narrow edgings, one piece of insertion and the end of a collar or cuff. This page differs from sheet 3 of the set of thirty-three issued by the museum in the 1980s. During conservation several samples had to be removed and placed on other sheets.

Points of interest

Line 2
2.c has an unusual footside. The two pairs between the whole stitch trails have been worked with a whole stitch in the middle and then worked with a catch stitch into the two trails.

Line 8 onwards
Include Bedfordshire laces.

Your challenge

Can you find the sample with Bucks point ground and Bedfordshire wheat-ear tallies?

Sheet 4

This page includes a mixture of Bucks point and Bedfordshire edgings. There are some interesting examples of gimp work forming and outlining patterns within the ground. Several samples were not on sheet 4 of the 1980s copies.

Points of interest

Line 1
1.a has a Mayflower filling hidden within the honeycomb filling. Turn the book and look at the design of 1.b. The edge becomes a flower with tallies as the stamen and a leaf below.

Your challenge

Can you find the nine-pin edging amongst the picots?

Sheet 5

There are 139 samples of narrow edgings sometimes known as 'baby laces' since they were used on this page. The samples vary in complexity and skill.

Points of interest

Lines 1-7
The fans have been worked in a thicker thread using only one bobbin passing through the passive pairs, whilst sample 7.d has been worked in the traditional way with a worker pair.

Lines 1 and 2
1.d and 2.b appear to be apple patterns.

Lines 12 and 13
12.h and 13.c are the sheep's head pattern.

Your challenge

Where are the spiders?

Sheet 6

There are 82 samples of edgings and two of insertions on this sheet. These types of narrow lace were used to trim underwear and baby clothes. The number of edgings and patterns on sheets 5 and 6 indicate the enormous demand for these products.

Points of interest

Line 2
2.e is the only sample on this page which incorporates Kat stitch.

Line 8
8.d has areas within the gimp that are worked in half stitch, which is unusual in English white lace and normally a feature of black lace.

Line 10
10.b does not incorporate a gimp around the whole stitch motif.

Your challenge

Find the cucumber footside.

Sheet 7

This sheet shows a variety of floral Bucks point edgings and one insertion. Note the variety of Mayflower fillings used in the grounds on this page.

Points of interest

Line 1
1.a look at the pointed edge. The passives have been taken into the headside. 1.b has a Mayflower design worked with whole stitch and pin chain.

Line 6
6.a and 6.c have Torchon spiders with the gimps.

Your challenge

Find the single piece of insertion amongst the edgings.

Sheet 8

The samples on this page are all Bedfordshire style and some of them appear to have been designed to enable the maker to work at speed. The traditional name for the long square leaf was plait and the plaits were known as legs.

Points of interest

Line 4
4.d incorporates kisses, two plaits crossing. There are other examples on this page.

Line 5
5.a has a four picot, Honiton filling.

Your challenge

Can you find the very fine example of double cucumber footside?

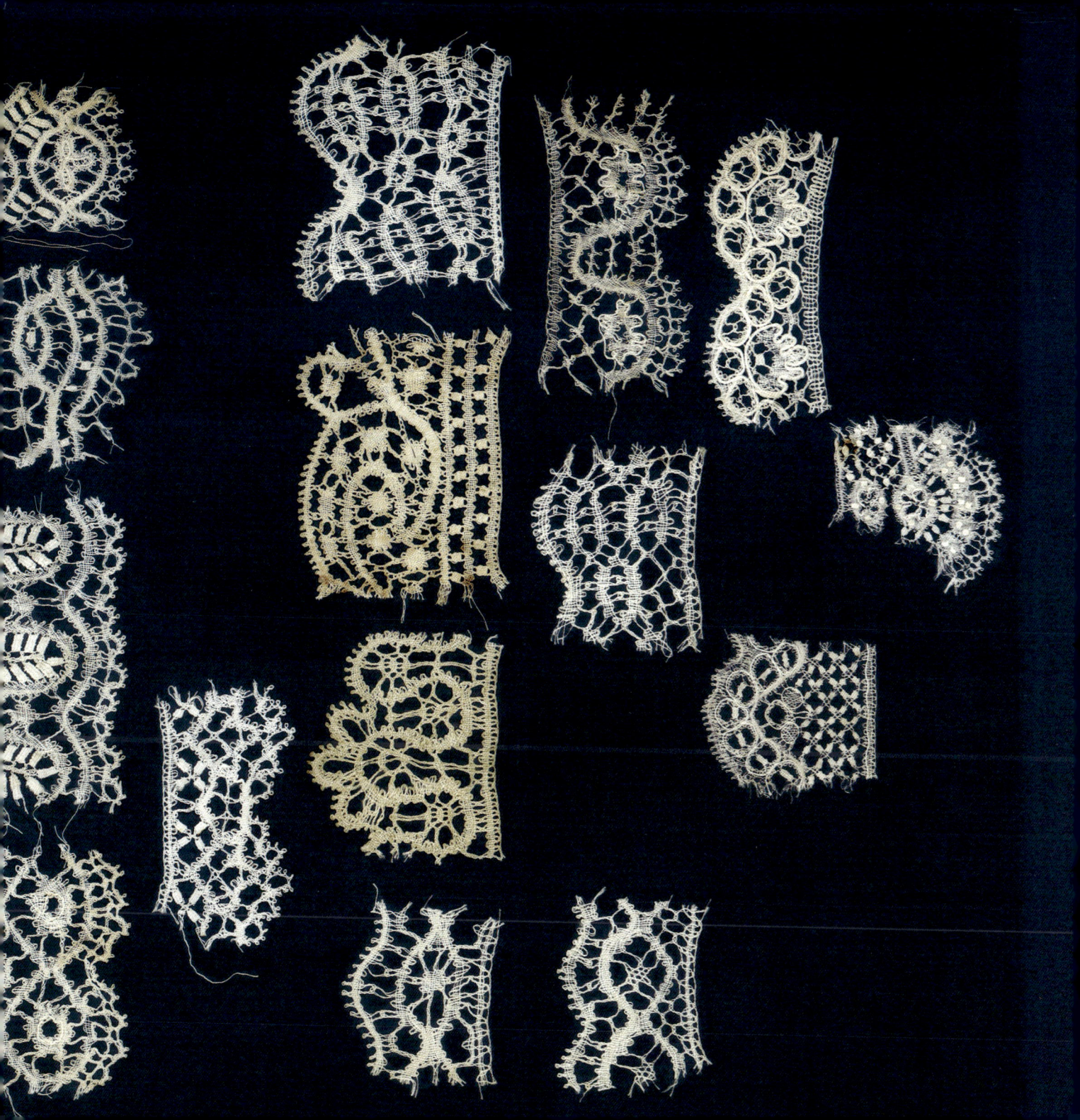

Sheet 9

All the samples on this page are made from Bedfordshire lace. They include a lappet or scarf end.

Points of interest

Lines 1 and 3
1.c, 3.c and 3.d all have a point ground.

Line 3
3.a has a honeycomb filling.
3.c is worked with a finer thread than 3.d and has a different footside. 3.c would have been faster to work than 3.d.

Line 4
4.c and 4.d are the same pattern both worked with the same thickness of thread, but probably by different lacemakers.

Your challenge

There are at least four variations of nine-pin edge on this page, can you find them?

Sheet 10

You may recognise some of the Buckinghamshire patterns on this page. Some designs have been turned into prickings by contemporary lacemakers and published in their books. The thick floss gimp in some samples gives the an impression of blonde lace styles.

Points of interest

Lines 1 and 2
1.c and 2.g do not have a footside edge making it easy to attach them to a machine made lace.

Line 3
3.c is a sample where the gimp thread forms a major part of the design.

On several lines a butterfly motif has been worked into the ground.

Your challenge

How many versions of the fern leaf pattern can you see?

Sheet 11

This page includes two lappet ends. Lappets were the long decorative ends attached to the side of ladies bonnets or caps. There are a variety of tallies amongst these samples, the square ones made before the introduction of Bedfordshire Maltese lace and the longer ones made after.

Points of interest

Lines 1 and 5
1.c has three pairs which go into a plait. Two pairs, and a twisted pair come out. The lappet 5.b is also worked in half stitch and has been made as a sample rather than being cut from a completed piece.

Line 4
4.c is an example of a coarse Bedfordshire insertion.

Your challenge

Find the shape with five legs, how is it achieved?

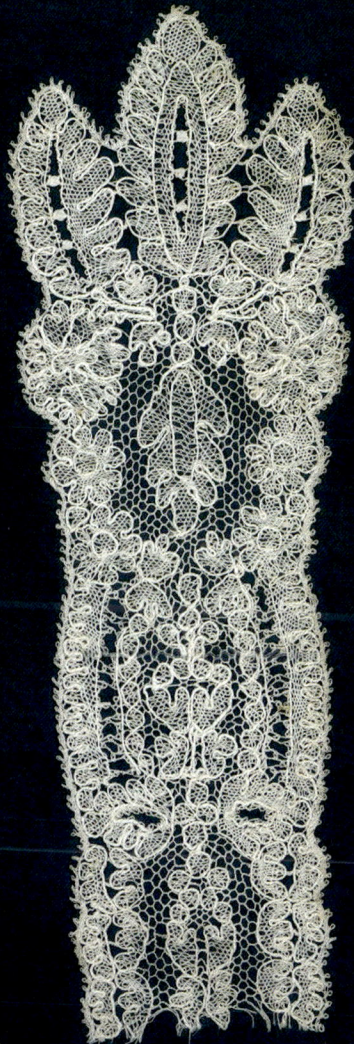

Sheet 12

There are many examples of Kat stitch, also known as wire ground on this page. Some of the fillings within the gimp threads have been worked in half stitch and several samples appear to have been made by the same person.

Points of interest

Line 1
1.d is the true lover's knot pattern.

Line 6
6.d has a pattern of a flower with two leaves at its base, but when edging was attached to a garment the design is upside down and looks rather like an angel.

Your challenge

Which patterns are similar to those of Chantilly lace?

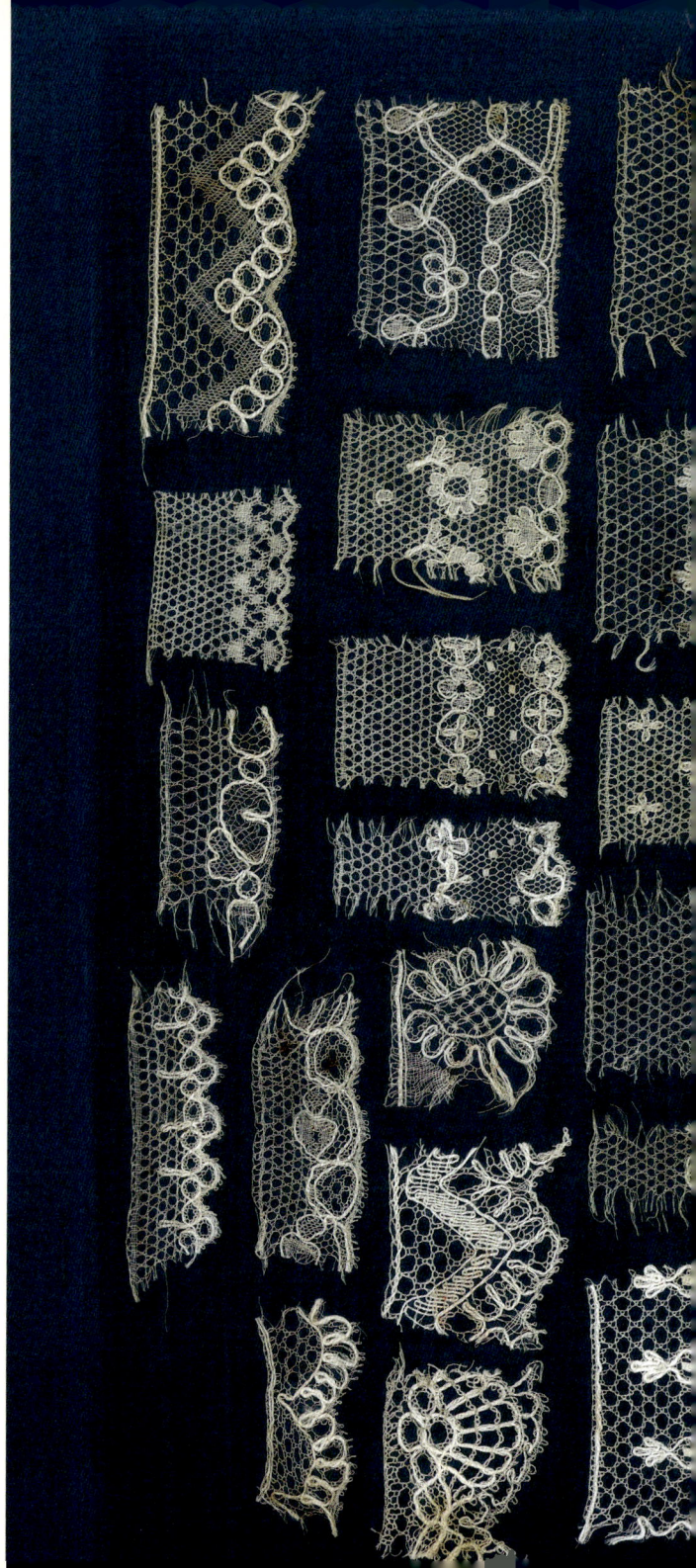

Sheet 13

Apart from the one piece of insertion on this page the remaining pieces are samples of collar, cuff or lappet ends. All of them appeared on the corresponding page in the original Pattern Book, but their positions have been changed during conservation.

Points of interest

Line 1
1.c has been worked in half stitch. 1.d has been worked in whole stitch.

Line 2
2.b is an interesting Bedfordshire pattern worked in very thick thread which gives it the appearance of a tape lace.

Your challenge

Can you find the tallies almost hidden within sample 2.b?

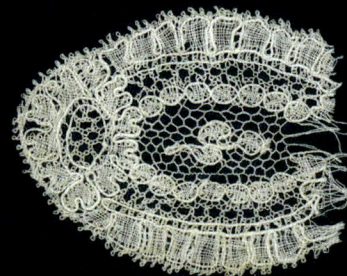

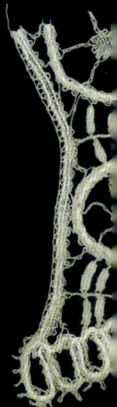

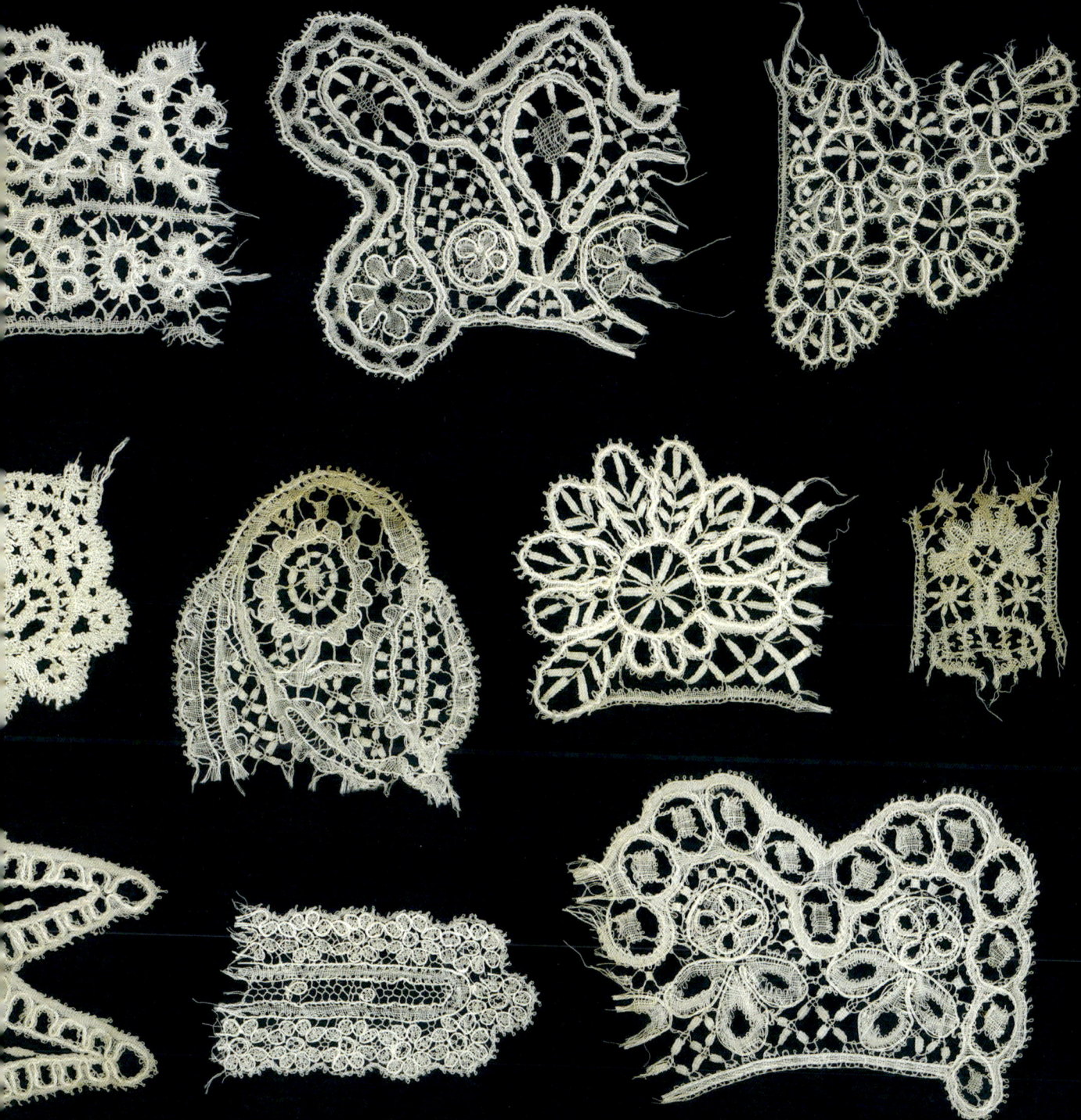

Sheet 14

A sheet of Bucks point edgings and three samples of lappets, including one very fine lappet worked with such a fine gimp thread it almost disappears into the dense pattern.

Points of interest

Lines 2, 3 and 4
Samples 2.a, 3.c and 4.a have been worked on a larger grid than the other samples making them faster to work.

Your challenge

Can you find the sample where either a pin hole has been missed during working or the picking was incorrect?

Sheet 15

There is a variation in quality within the Bucks point edgings on this page, suggesting that some may have been made much later in the 1800s than others. This page has been altered from that of the 1980s publication of the sample book.

Points of interest

Line 3
3.e has large spaces in the ground.

Line 4
4.e has been worked on a larger grid. 4.f does not have a footside.

Line 8
8.f has a cucumber footside.

Line 9
9.a has a double cucumber footside.

Your challenge

Can you find the sample where the quality of the headside does not match the ground and footside?

Sheet 16

This sheet contains Bedfordshire lace edgings of various widths, one piece of insertion lace and a collar or cuff end.

Points of interest

Line 1
1.b is made from a thicker thread and the heavy lace may have been used to trim household linens. The footside is Cluny, with a kiss and the leaves are Cluny style.

Line 3
3.a is the only insertion on the page. 3.d is a sample for a collar or cuff.

Your challenge

Look for the variety of nine-pin edges within the samples on this sheet.

Sheet 17

Fifty-two samples of Bucks point edgings fill this sheet. There is a variation in quality once again indicating a possible variation in dates of making. This page does not include all the samples shown on the same sheet in the 1980s publication. During conservation some samples were moved to the additional sheets.

Points of interest

Lines 2 and 6
2.d and 6.a are similar designs but one has an open centre to the diamond.

Line 6
6.e. This design is similar to one known as The Bride.

Line 8
8.a The design looks like a butterfly motif.

Your challenge

Can you find the samples with honeycomb filling?

Sheet 18

Just one row of edgings with Kat stitch ground interrupts this page of Bucks point edgings. The samples are dominated by arrangements of tallies, or dots, in the ground.

Points of interest

Line 9
9.b, 9.c and 9.g. The areas of cloth stitch are worked without a gimp outline making the pattern less obvious than others on the page. 9.f has a flower and circles worked into the ground.

Your challenge

Can you find one edging with a prominent design does not have a footside?

Sheet 19

The Bucks point edgings on this sheet have comparatively little ground in comparison to the area of pattern. This page was on the reverse of page 1 in the original Pattern Book donated by Thomas Wyatt Bagshawe.

Points of interest

Lines 3 and 4
Very often the pattern works best when the edging is attached to stand upwards rather than downwards. 3.b is an example where the design possibly a bunch of grapes works well when hanging downwards. 4.b is less successful as the flower motif is less obvious.

Your challenge

Find the samples where the tallies enhance the pattern?

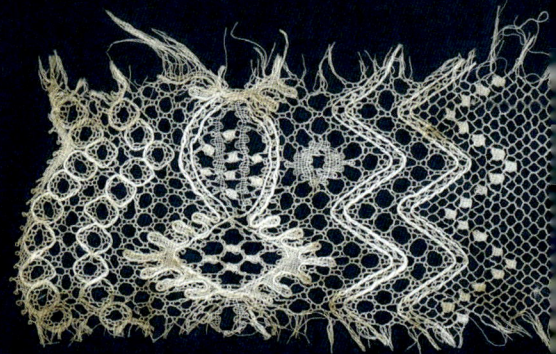

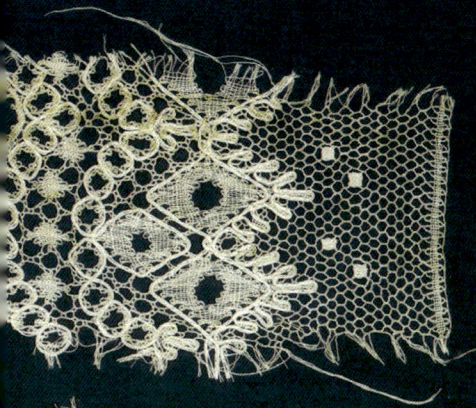

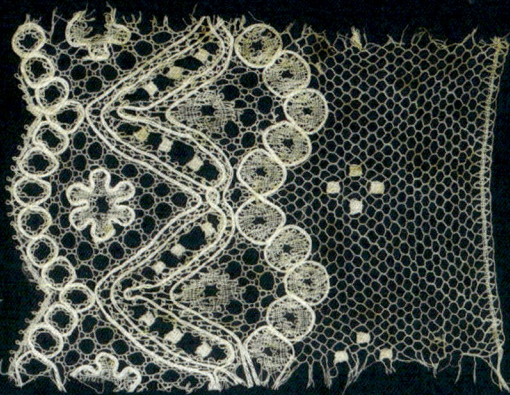

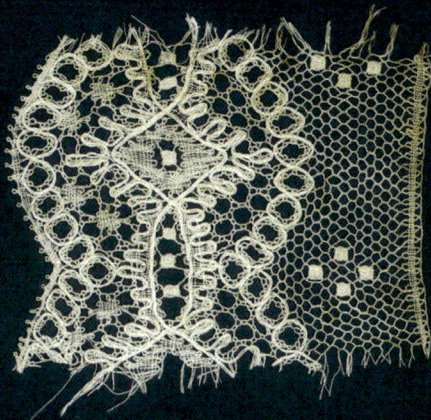

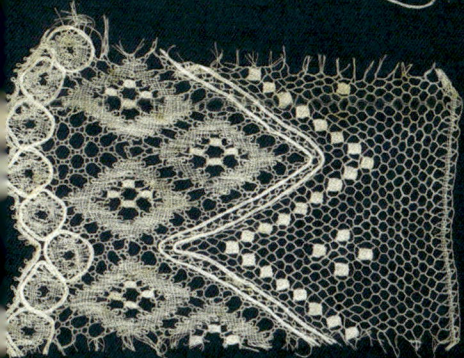

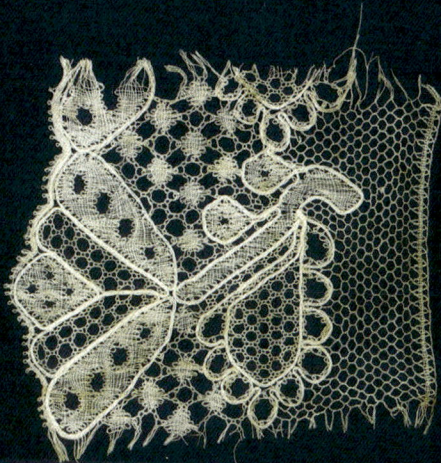

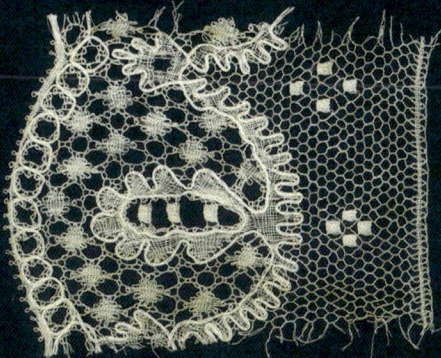

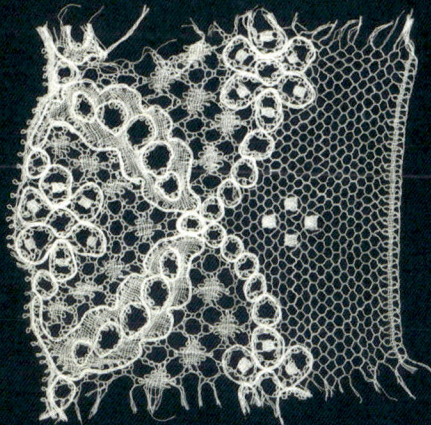

Sheet 20

There is a mixture of Bucks point and Bedfordshire patterns on this sheet which was originally on the reverse of page 2 in the Lace Dealer's Pattern Book.

Points of interest

Line 3
3.b Honeycomb filling has been used to great effect along the edge of this pattern. Both 3.a and 3.b are very fine work.

Line 4
4.b note how spiders have been used in place of six-plait crossing.

Your challenge

Look for the wheel motifs with the unusual centres.

Sheet 21

This is the first sheet entirely comprising Bucks point insertion samples. The samples show a wide range of pattern design. Some may have been designed by the same person, and some may have been made by the same lacemakers. This sheet was originally on the reverse of page 3 of the Lace Dealer's Pattern Book.

Points of interest

Lines 1, 3, 4 and 7
1.d, 3.d, 4.c and 7.a have no footside which probably indicates they were designed to be inserted into net.

Line 2
2.e is the original version of a modern motif called butterfly.

Line 4
4.e is the original version of a modern variation called Butterflies.

Your challenge

Can you find the Royal connection?

Sheet 22

This sheet of highly decorative Bucks point edgings was on the reverse of page 4 of the original Lace Dealer's Pattern Book. During conservation the samples were moved from their positions on the original page.

Points of interest

Lines 1, 2 and 3
In samples 1.d, 2.a and 3.d note the number of pairs taken into the headside valley, they are worked as needed in the 'ups'.

Line 1
1.b incorporates Bedfordshire leaves in its design.

Line 3
3.c has a pin chain in the central motif.

Line 4
4.a contains an eagle differs from the previous one on sample sheet 22. This sample has a more complex filling that incorporates tallies. It is also more neatly executed.

Your challenge

Look for the eagle.

Sheet 23

The Bucks point edgings and one piece of insertion were on the reverse of page 5 in the original Lace Dealer's Pattern Book. During conservation the samples were moved from their positions in the original sample book.

Points of interest

Line 4
4.e has a Valenciennes ground.

Line 6
6.d has a nine-pin edge and Valenciennes ground added to a piece of Bucks point. The gimp on this sample is a tightly twisted thread in place of the usual soft, loose or untwisted thread.

Your challenge

Can you see the 'baby lace'?

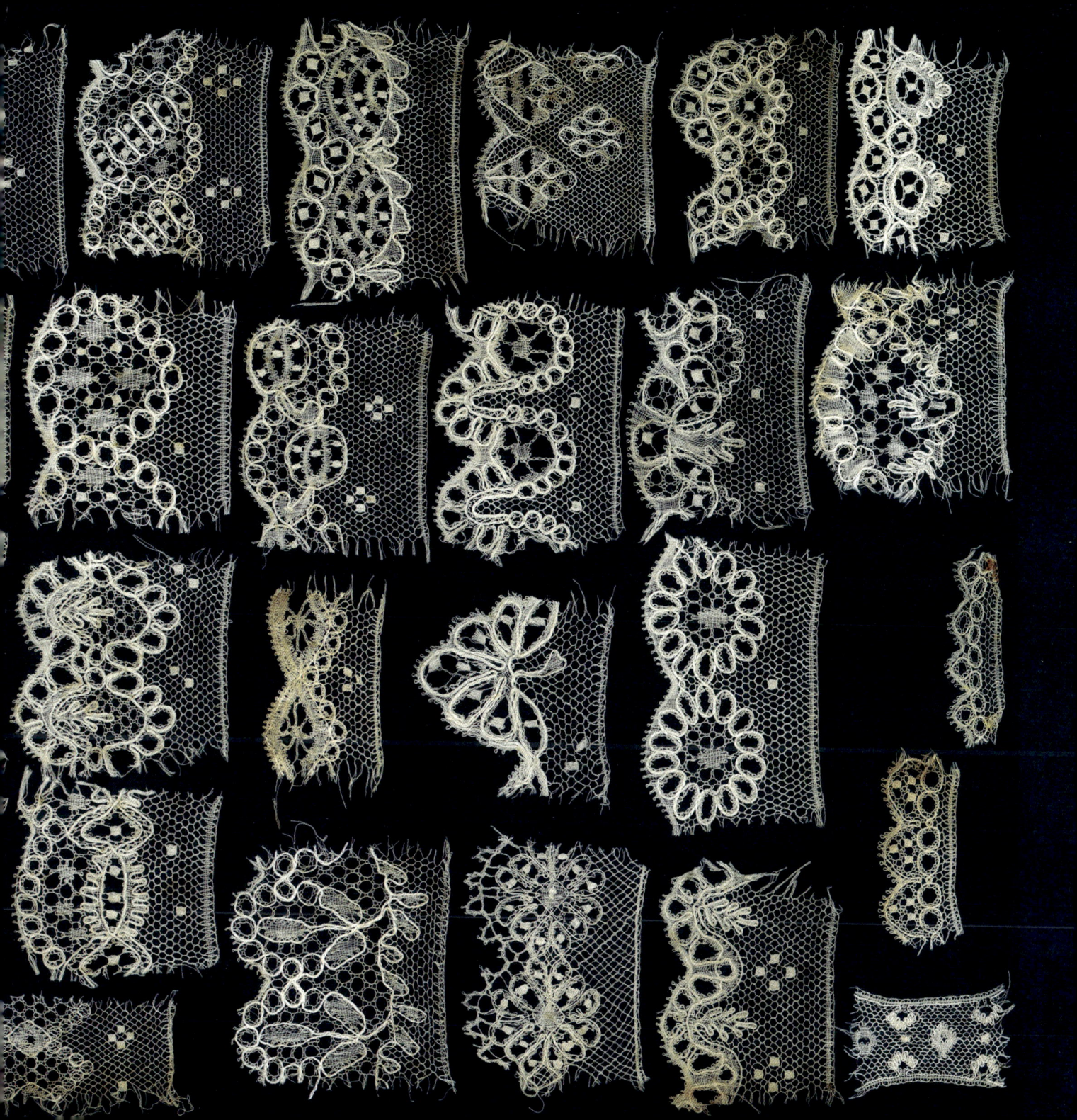

Sheet 24

There are 107 samples of narrow Bucks point edgings, sometimes called 'baby lace'. This sheet was originally the reverse of page 6 in the Lace Dealer's Pattern Book.

Points of interest

Lines 1 and 5
1.e and 5.e are the same pattern.

Lines 6 and 13
6.a and 13.d have heavy gimp threads passing along the footside.

Line 18
18.e has a double cucumber footside.

Your challenge

Find the heart and ring pattern.

Sheet 25

A mixture of Bucks point edgings, insertions, a lappet end and two collar ends fill this sheet. This page was originally the reverse of page 7 in the Lace Dealer's Pattern Book. During conservation seven samples from other pages were added to this sheet.

Points of interest

Lines 3 and 4
3.a has a pattern design which combines Bucks point and Bedfordshire laces, whereas the collar end, 4.a is entirely Bucks point.

Line 5
5.a is a lappet with a Bedfordshire design, nine-pin edge and Bucks point centre panel.

Your challenge

Look for the unusual honeycomb ground used in place of the more common type.

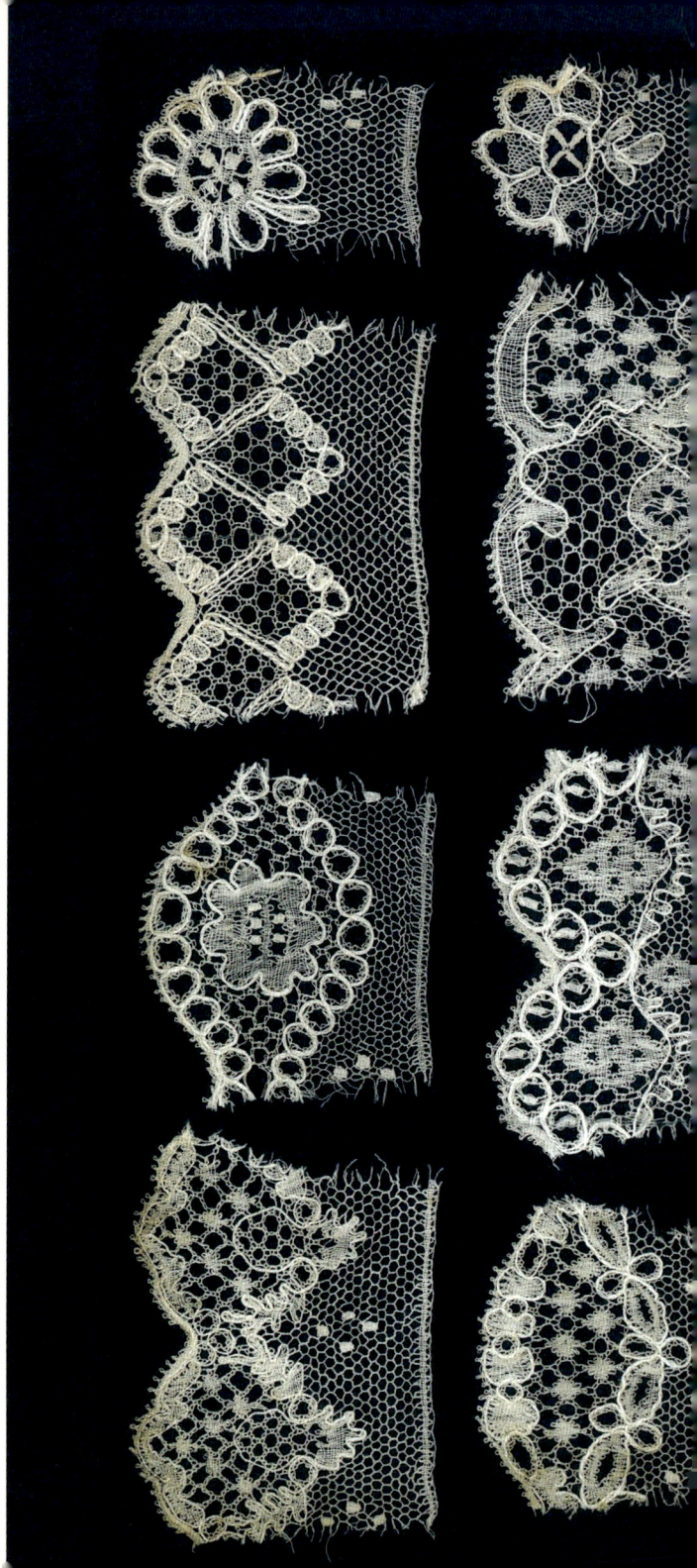

Sheet 26

This sheet contains Bedfordshire samples, some with nine-pin edge and some with a picot edge. Note the variety of patterns and length of some of the wheatears. This sheet was originally the reverse of page 8 in the original Pattern Book.

Points of interest

Line 3
3.a is a sample that has a filling of Bucks point in the design.

Lines 3 and 4
3.b and 4.a are the same patterns worked in different threads.

Your challenge

Look for the variations in the footside patterns.

Sheet 27

On this sheet there is a selection of Bucks point edgings including one elaborate wide piece. These samples must have been made by experienced workers. This sheet was originally the reverse of page 9 in the Lace Dealer's Pattern Book.

Points of interest

Line 1
1.b has a Honiton filling known as six-pin chain and leads.

Line 4
4.a contains an eagle that differs from the previous one on sheet 22. This sample has a more complex filling that incorporates tallies. It is also more neatly executed.

Your challenge

Look for the unusual flower centres.

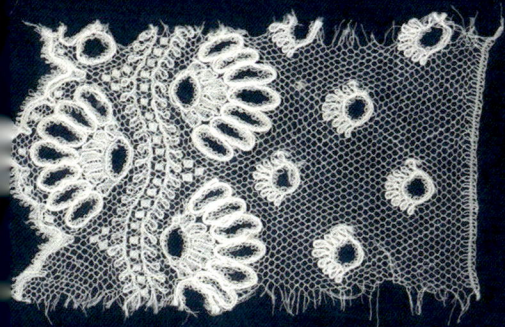

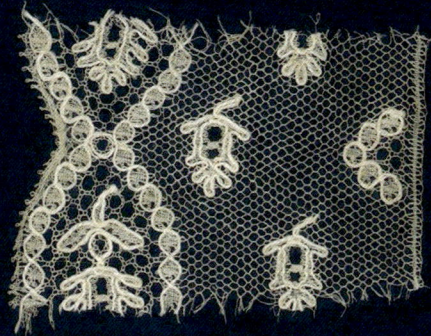

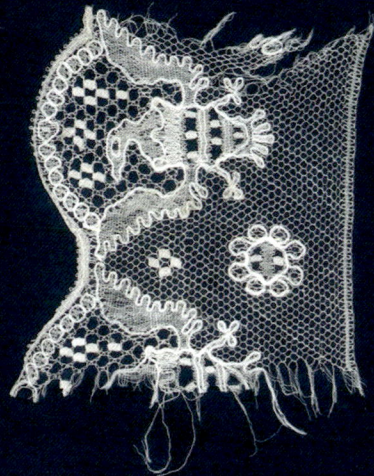

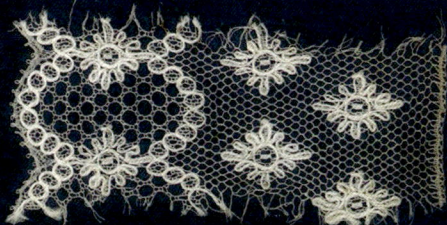

Sheet 28

Lacemakers have made prickings from some of these Bucks point edgings and you will find them in modern lace books. This sheet was originally the reverse of page 10 in the Lace Dealer's Pattern Book. The samples have been moved from their original positions and some added from other sheets during conservation.

Points of interest

Lines 2, 3, 5 and 6
2.a, 3.b, 5.b, 6.b and 6.d are samples that have been worked on a larger grid and have larger open spaces in the flower petals making them similar to Blonde lace designs.

Your challenge

Can you find the running river pattern?

Sheet 29

A mixture of Bedfordshire wide, narrow edgings and one lappet end. This sheet was originally the reverse of page 11 in the Lace Dealer's Pattern Book. One sample was removed from the original page and one added to this sheet during conservation.

Points of interest

Line 1
1.c. Could this be a Thomas Lester design? It is elaborately floral which is regarded as the style of the Lesters.

Line 2
2.a has a spider's web made with pin chain ground. In sample 2.c look at the novel way that tallies have been used to make a square.

Line 5
5.c is the only sample of Bucks point on this sheet.

Your challenge

Look for the Cluny and spider's web footside.

Sheet 30

This is the second sheet containing samples of Kat stitch. These patterns would often be used for making black lace and incorporate a lot of half stitch. There are several pattern duplicates. Originally this page was the reverse of page 12 in the Lace Dealer's Pattern Book. Half stitch has been worked into samples on each line.

Points of interest

Line 3
3.a, 3.b and 3.d are the same pattern with some differences. In 3.a the pattern is reversed.

Line 4
4.c and 4.d are the same patterns, but seem to be reversed rather than one being mounted with the front showing and the other with the back showing.

Your challenge

Can you find three samples of the same pattern that include different numbers of passives in the footside?

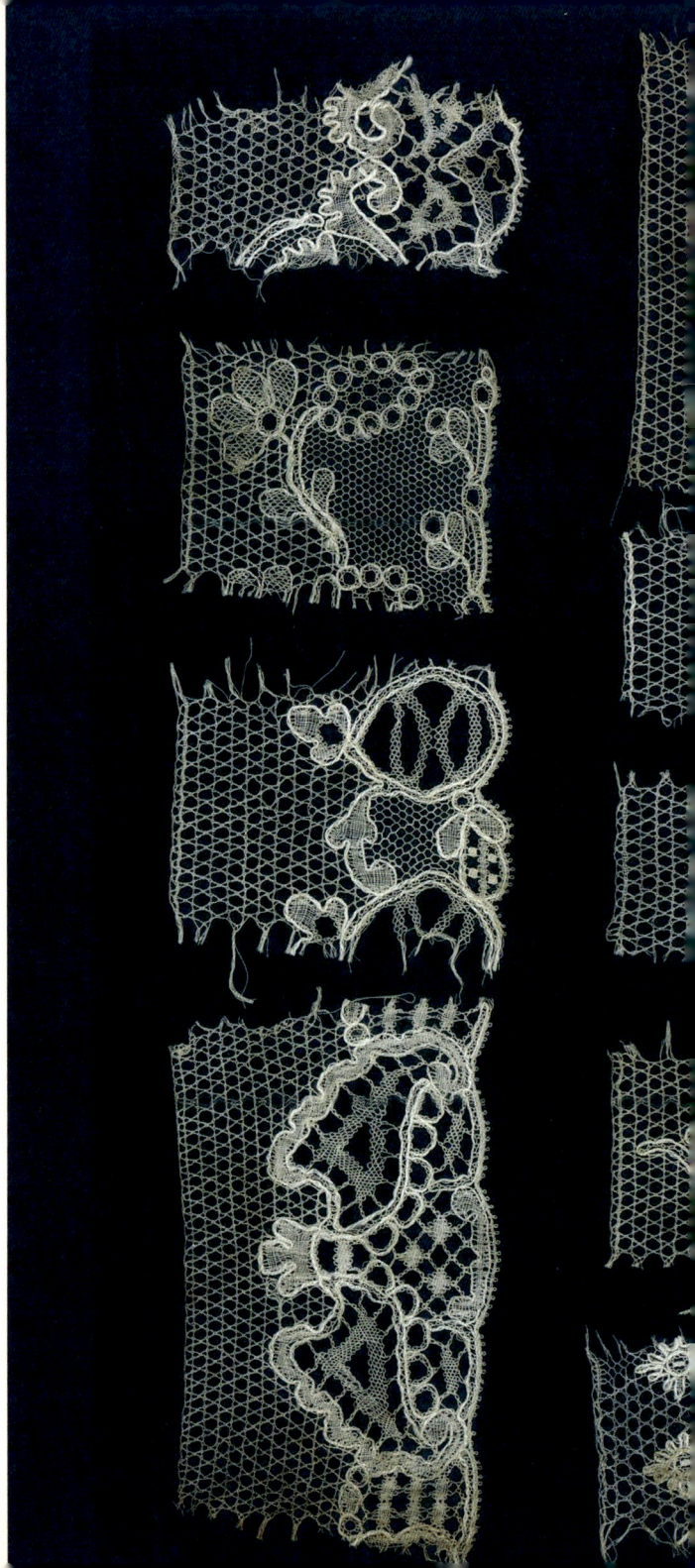

Sheet 31

This sheet contains samples of Bedfordshire edgings made by makers with different skill levels. They have worked within their capabilities to include some interesting features. This page was the reverse of page 13 in the original Pattern book.

Points of interest

Lines 3 and 5
3.c and 5.c have long double nine-pin edges, and the plaits are loose.

Line 4
4.a has an unusual change in the headside.

Line 5
5.b incorporates a row of neat kisses within the headside.

Your challenge

Can you find the unusual trails of tallies in two samples?

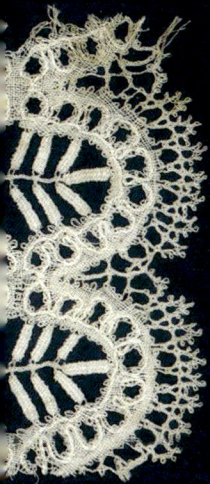

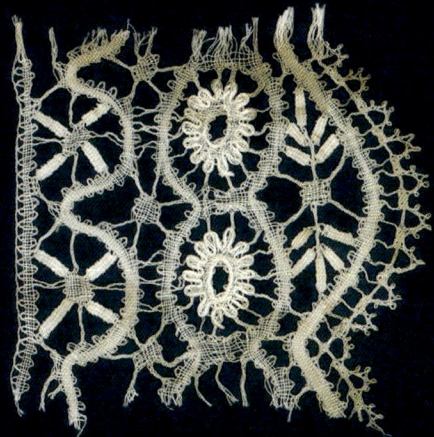

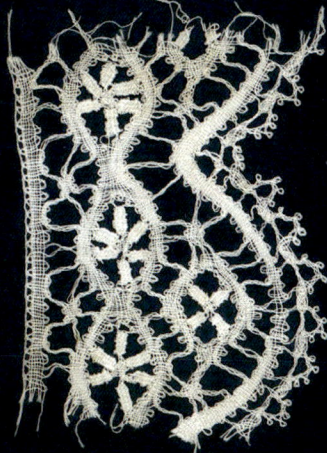

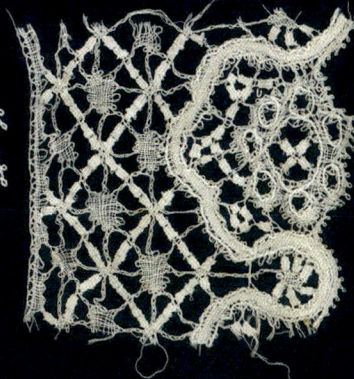

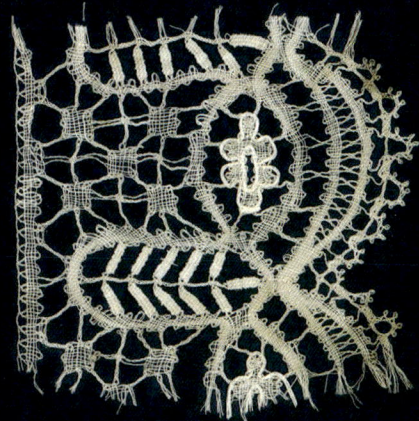

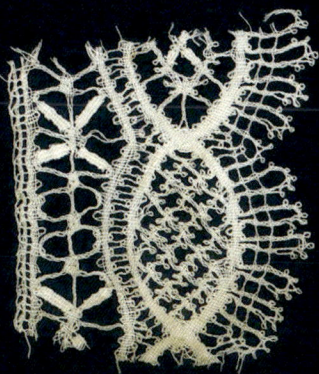

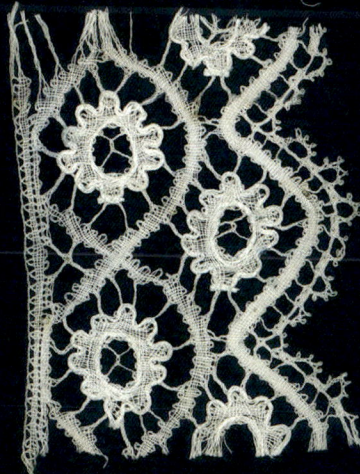

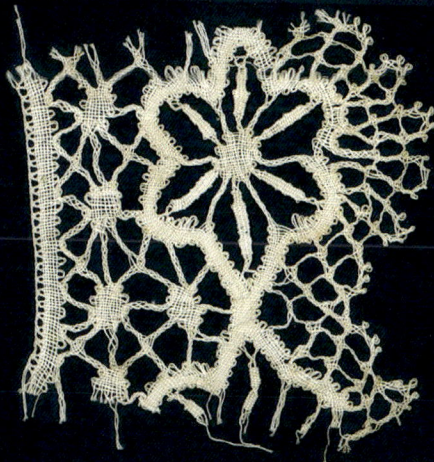

Sheet 32

Bucks point edgings fill this sheet. This page was the reverse of page 14 in the original Lace Dealer's Pattern Book. Whilst all the samples which were on the original page are on this sheet their order has been slightly changed.

Points of interest

Lines 1 and 2
1.d and 2.d are the same pattern. 2.d looks more dense because it has been worked with a thicker thread.

Lines 1 and 4
1.a and 4.c are the same pattern made to look different by moving the position of the gimp thread around the honeycomb rings.

Your challenge

Find the sample with a honeycombe trail.

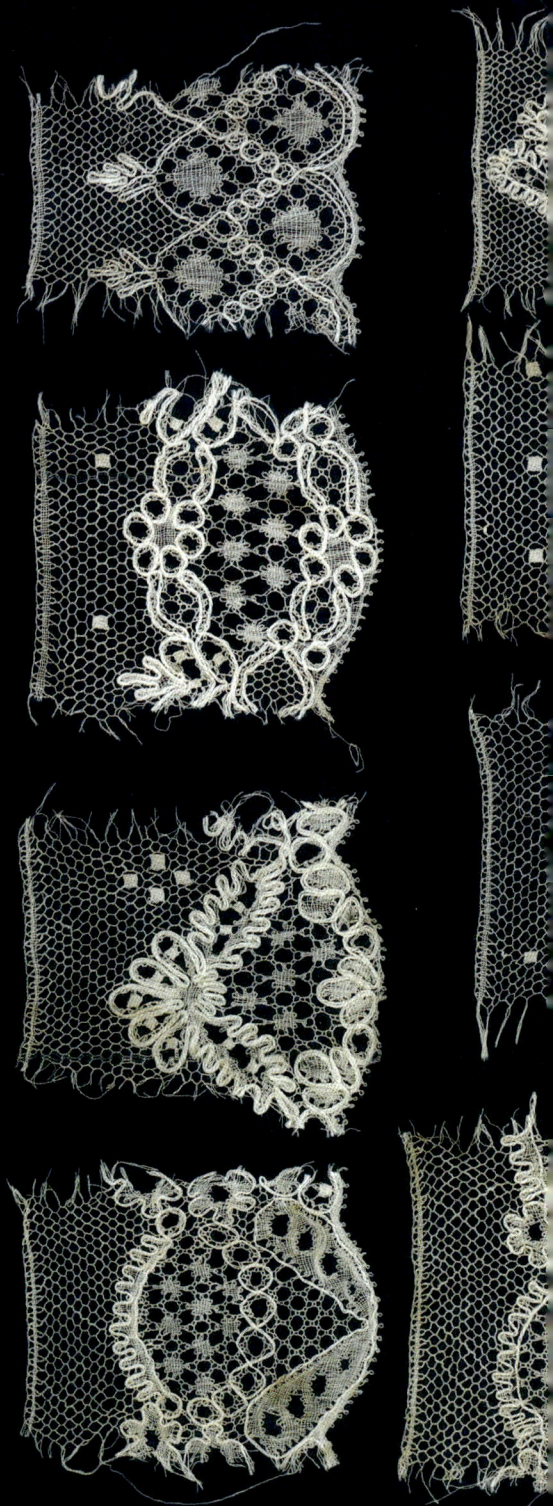

Sheet 33

These very fine Bucks point edgings are probably some of the earliest in this book. They are expertly and precisely made. This page was the reverse of page 18 in the original Lace Dealer's Pattern Book. Three samples were removed from the original page and repositioned on other sheets.

Points of interest

Line 3
3.d has a pin-chain filling.

Line 4
4.g has an unusual whole stitch diamond in that the gimp follows the steps rather than being pulled straight.

Lines 6 and 7
6.d and 7.e are two samples made by experienced lacemakers. Note the large areas of cloth stitch.

Your challenge

Can you find the sample without a footside?

Sheet 34

From this point onwards the sheets contain samples which had either become detached from the original Lace Dealer's Pattern Book, or are those which have been repositioned from their original pages during conservation. This sheet contains some beautiful Bedfordshire lace amongst the Bucks point edgings.

Points of interest

Line 5
5.b is also found on sheet 32, 5.a. Several samples on this sheet are repeated on different sheets throughout the book. 5.c is interesting as tallies and plaits have been combined to make the flowers.

Your challenge

Can you find the sample with a kiss in the middle of the flower?

Sheet 35

Bedfordshire and Cluny insertions feature on this sheet. Cluny was used to decorate household linens, as it was quick to make. By pulling a thread in the footside Bedfordshire edgings could be gathered into a curve.

Points of interest

Line 1
1.d is a wide edging that includes legs and a honeycomb filling within the pattern.

Line 4
4.a is a very unusual insertion which was simple and quick to make. This sample is in the style of Cluny.

Your challenge

Find the edging with a very unusual footside incorporating raised tallies.

Sheet 36

This sheet contains Bucks point edgings, insertions and two samples of Bedfordshire lace. The quality of the samples shows great variation probably indicating that some were made much earlier than others. Some samples are made from such fine thread and required tiny pins that it is probably not possible to replicate them today.

Points of interest

Line 1
1.a is a variation of a little fan pattern.

Lines 8 and 11
8.b and 8.c do not have a footside. 11.b does not have a footside and the gimp passes through the edge.

Your challenge

Can you see the Torchon spider in the middle of the motif?

Sheet 37

Bucks point edgings fill this sheet. There is a variation in the quality of making and thickness of threads used within the samples on this sheet and some samples appear quite untidy.

Points of interest

Line 1
1.b has gimp thread used in place of whole stitch.

Line 9
9.b has a net that changes halfway along this sample and the ground inserted into the motif is worked on a different angle. 9.e is a mixture of Bucks point and Bedfordshire styles.

Your challenge

Can you find the sample which copies the style of Blonde lace?

Sheet 38

This sheet has a mixture of Bucks Point edgings and insertions, two pieces of Bedfordshire lace and two lappet ends. The lappets have been worked entirely in half stitch.

Points of interest

Lines 2 and 5
2.c, right hand piece and 5.a are both made with fine thread but have unusually thick gimps. There is a similarly thick gimp on sheet 37. Could the gimp be a double thread wound onto the bobbin?

Line 3
3.a is made from very fine thread and has been expertly worked.

Your challenge

Look for the sample of insertion that has Vandyke edges.

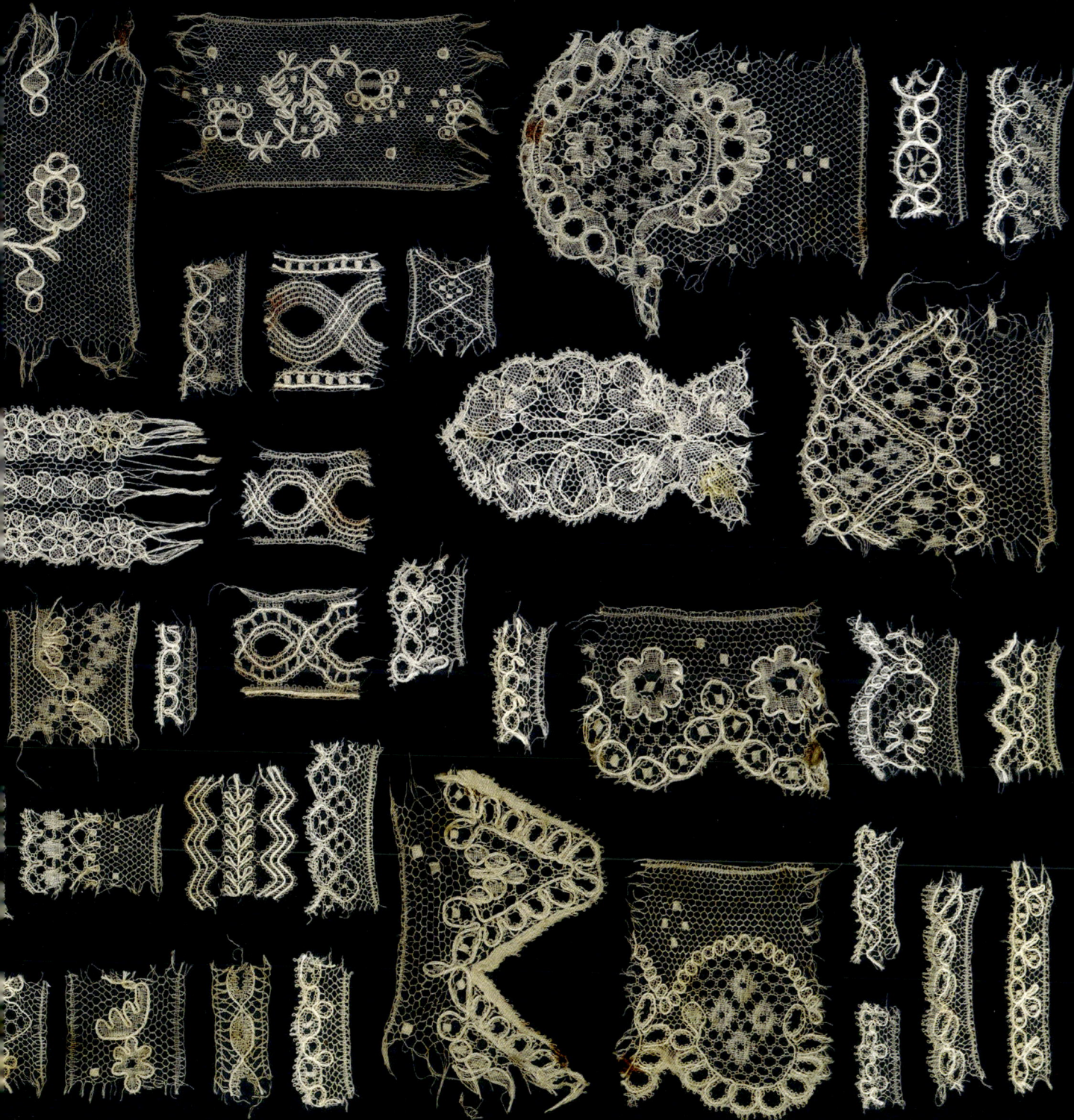

Sheet 39

Bucks Point edgings, two samples of insertion, a lappet end and one Bedfordshire collar end are on this sheet. There are also two pieces of 'baby lace'.

Points of interest

Line 1
1.a does not have a footside.

Line 4
4.b is a collar end with an interesting mix of Bucks point detail and Bedfordshire techniques.

Line 6
6.b is interesting as the maker has used two thicknesses of thread for the gimp, a thicker one on the head edge and narrower in the body.

Your challenge

Look for the insertion with a gimp thread on both edges.

Sheet 40

Most of these samples of Bucks point lace made with black thread have half stitch ground to give the lace a lighter appearance. There are two pieces of Bedfordshire on the sheet and a narrow lappet end.

Points of interest

Line 4
4.b is an insertion with a Vandyke edge that incorporates Bucks point lace techniques and a fine gimp, but it is not obviously Bucks point.

Line 6
6.a is an interesting sample of insertion with two patterned edges outlined in a thick gimp thread.

Your challenge

Two samples have the same pattern, can you find them?

Sheet 41

This second sheet of black lace samples includes a range of edgings. All are made with half stitch which is a characteristic feature of black lace.

Points of interest

Lines 1 and 2
1.b and 2.b may have been made to attach to net as they do not have a footside. Sample 1.b does not have picots on its footside even though the pattern runs along its edge.

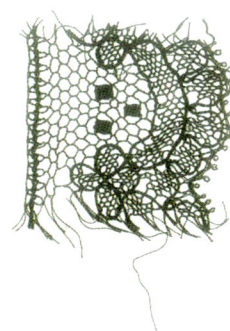

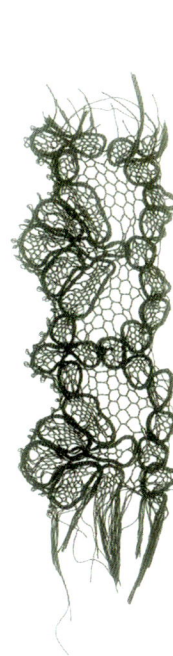

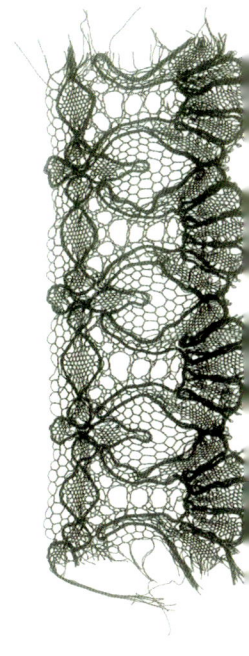

Your challenge

Can you find the two samples that also appear on sample sheet 40?

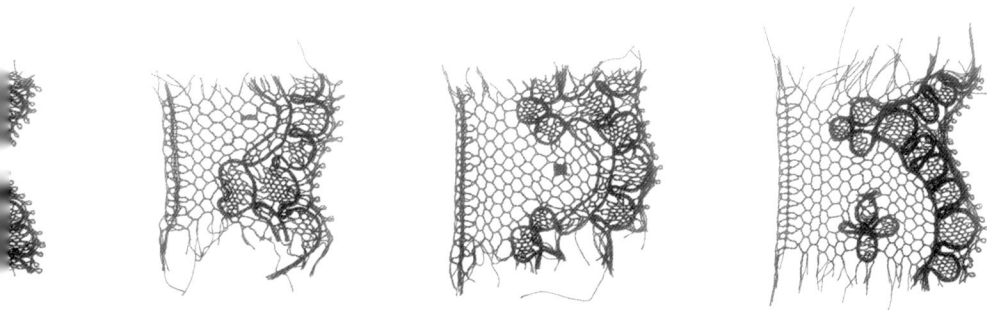

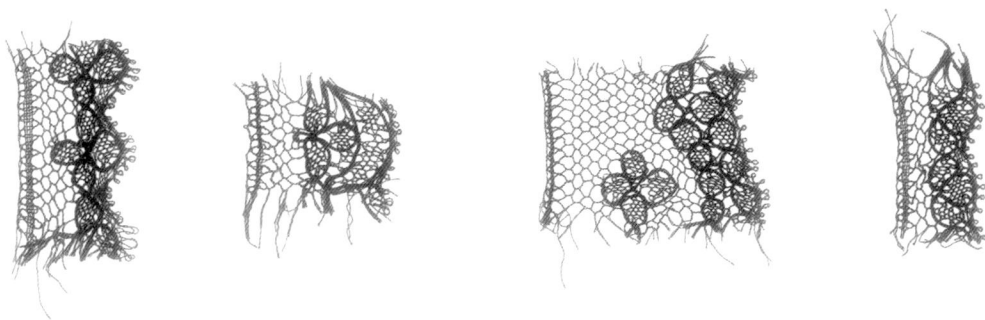

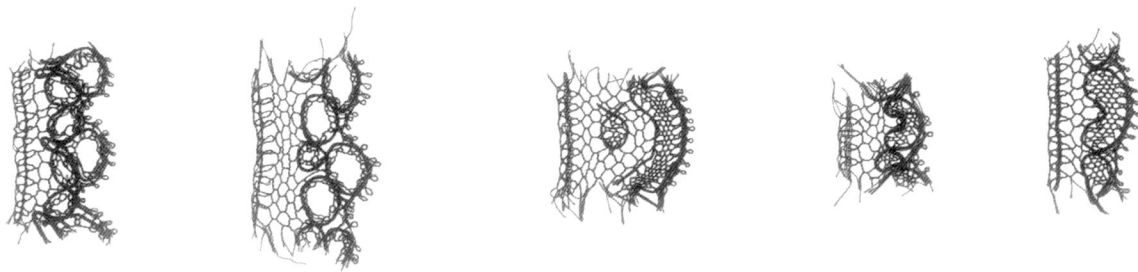

Sheet 42

These are the six samples which were contained in an envelope then mounted onto this sheet during conservation. The samples probably became detached from the original Pattern Book during its years of use.

Points of interest

Line 1
1.c is the third example of the eagle design and is possibly the best. The other two eagle motifs are on sheets 22 and 27. All three are different.

Line 2
2.a is sample of black lace that is probably machine made as the stitches are so even.

Your challenge

One sample has a raised tally in the middle of a circular motif, can you find it?

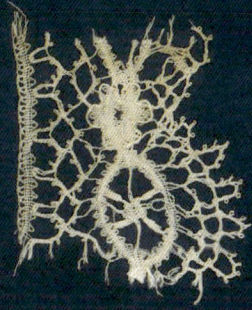

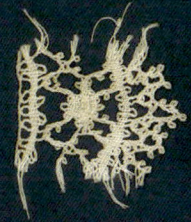

List of Original Donors

The conservation project could not have been undertaken without the help and support of the Lacemakers' Circle and lacemaking groups and individuals worldwide whose combined efforts financed the 1998 publication and also provided much useful advice.

The following list records those who raised money for the conservation appeal:

Individuals

Mrs M Allen	Miss H Gannac	Mrs C & Mr P Prentis
Mrs M Bartholomew	Mrs I Gentle	Mrs A Quinn
Ms J Beasley	Mrs D Glasspool	Ms T Raffner
Mrs Berryman & students	Miss K Gorman	Ms M Rogers
Mrs B Billington	Mrs M Green	Mrs T Sargent
Mrs M Body	Mrs P Hallam	Mrs B Savagar
Mrs A Bone	Miss M Hollingsworth	Miss J Sayers
Mrs P Bramwell	Mr W Hornsby	Mrs D Smith
Mrs J Chinn	Mrs S Jackson	Mrs K Smith
Miss P Chittell	Mrs C Johnston	Miss P Smith
Mrs E Coom	Ms L Jones	Ms J Stinison
Mrs J Cornford	Ms D Lillevig	Ms G Stott
Mrs J Cottrill	Mrs P Lloyd	Mr A Taylor
Miss L Cumming	Mrs H McShane	Mrs E Taylors & students
Mrs D Darvill	Mrs P Martin	Mrs M Walker
Mr D Davis	Miss A Monteith	Mrs E Wall
Ms J Draper	Mrs H Neaverson	Mrs E Whetton
Miss A Duxbury	Mrs P Nichols	Mrs E Wood
Mrs J Edis	Mrs G Patchell	
Mrs O Evans	Mrs K Piano	

Organisations

Arachne
Australia Lacemakers
Barwell Lacemakers
Bon Accord Lacemakers
The Braid Society
Bromley Lacemakers
Burwell Lacemakers
Carillon Lacemakers
Chesterton Lacemakers
Chipping Sodbury Lacemakers
Cleddau Lacemakers
Essex Lacemakers
Gipping Valley Lacemakers
Haven Lacemakers
Hilllingdon Lace Thumpers
Inspired Lacemakers, Chesterfield
Irthlingborough Lace & Craft Group
The Lace Friends of Luton Museum
The Lacemakers' Circle
Lacemakers of Warwickshire
Leicestershire Bobbin Lace Guild

McDougal Lacemakers
Moray Lacemakers
Mount Elija Lace Club
New Zealand Lace Society
Newbury Bobbins
Norfolk Lacemakers
Nottinghamshire Bobbin Lace Society
Rhondda Lacemakers
Ridgeway Lacemakers
Riverside Lacemakers
Stotfold Lacemakers
Suffolk Lacemakers
Taylor Made (Printers)
Tylehurst Lace Guild
Wantage Lacemakers
Watford Lacemakers
West Oxfordshire Lacemakers
1066 Lacemakers

Every effort has been made to ensure that this list is accurate and comprehensive. Luton Culture apologises for any possible errors or omissions.

Further Reading

Several well-known Lacemakers have used the Lace Dealer's Pattern Book as a source for creating prickings. The following list includes just some of the publications that have included designs created from the samples.

If you are able to add further titles to the list we would be delighted to hear from you.

100 Traditional Bobbin Lace Patterns
Geraldine Stott, Bridget Cook
Batsford, 1982
ISBN: 0 7134 3926 2

Bedfordshire Lace Making
Pamela Nottingham
Batsford, 1992
ISBN: 0 86417 500 0

Bucks Point Prickings
Kate Riley
Lace Guild, 1999
ISBN: 1 901372 06 5

Pillow Lace Book 5
Margaret Hamer, Kathleen Waller
Self-published, 1979

Pillow Lace Book 6
Margaret Hamer, Kathleen Waller
Self-published, 1980

The Technique of Bucks Point Lace
Pamela Nottingham
Batsford, 1981
ISBN: 0 7134 2175 4

**Thomas Lester, his Lace and the
East Midlands Industry 1820-1905**
Ann Buck
Ruth Bean, 1981
ISBN: 0 903585 09 X

Your challenge – the answers

The techniques used to create lace patterns varied between counties and professional lacemakers. Their methods are sometimes a little different from the techniques used today. Today's lacemakers often use different terminology to talk about a particular design feature. Do you agree with our answers?

Sheet 1
5.c

Sheet 2
1.a, 2.b, 4.a, 7.e

Sheet 3
13.a, 14.a

Sheet 4
2.b

Sheet 5
2.e, 4.g

Sheet 6
1.b

Sheet 7
4.d

Sheet 8
4.b

Sheet 9
2.a, 2.b, 7.c, 8.b

Sheet 10
1.c, 3.c, 4.c, 7.e, 9.c

Sheet 11
1.c

Sheet 12
8.b, 8.c

Sheet 13
Did you find the tallies?

Sheet 14
4.c

Sheet15
8.b

Sheet 16
How many variations
did you find?

Sheet 17
2.e, 3.c, 4.a, 5.b,c,d,e,
6.d,e, 7.b,c, 8.e, 9.c,d,e
10.a,b,c, d 11.b,d,e.
11.d is a good example.

Sheet 18
8.g

Sheet 19
1.a, 2.b

Sheet 20
6.a

Sheet 21
7.h. A crown

Sheet 22
6.d

Sheet 23
Lines 1 and 8

Sheet 24
10.f

Sheet 25
3.d

Sheet 26
Look in particular at 2.d
and 4.a

Sheet 27
1.c has leads,2.c has
honeycomb, 4.a and
4.b have whole stitch
and tallies.

Sheet 28
4.d

Sheet 29
3.c

Sheet 30
3.a, 3.b,3.d

Sheet 31
1.b and 4.b

Sheet 32
4.c

Sheet 33
6.c

Sheet 34
1.b

Sheet 35
4.a

Sheet 36
7.a

Sheet 37
1.b

Sheet 38
3.e left hand sample

Sheet 39
6.a

Sheet 40
2.d and 7.c

Sheet 41
6.c and 3.d on
sheet 40 4.a and
5.b on sheet 40

Sheet 42
1.b

For your notes or samples

For your notes or samples

The DVD accompanying this book allows detailed viewing of each sheet. This will enable greater understanding of the original techniques and appreciation of the lacemakers' skills. The DVD contains both jpeg and pdf images. There is also a folder containing digital images for your personal use in non-commercial publications and websites. Our intention in providing this facility is to benefit knowledge and awareness of lace.

The background colour on the DVD represents the original colour of the card mounts used for conservation, whilst the background colour throughout the book has been darkened to enhance viewing of the lace.

The DVD is protected by copyright.